Limited Edition No. _____/4,669,732

DEDICATION

This book is dedicated to all you golfers who have ever fiddled scorecards, lied about handicaps, quietly improved a lie, disguised an airshot as a practice swing or bored someone in the 19th . . . (that should catch just about all of you).

Written by: Peter Sherwood and Gary Alderdice

Editor: Peter Sherwood

Illustrations and Graphic Design: Roy Bisson

Enquiries, complaints, writs, evasions, paternity suits, libels, disclaimers, reproduction fees, apologies, palimony proceedings — all in Chinese script please with pre-paid return envelope to
Lincoln Green Publishing, 19th floor, Tai Sang Commercial Building, 24 Hennessy Road, Hong Kong.

ISBN 962-7028-16-9

Other books in this series include:

The World's Best Horseracing Book Ever
The World's Best Tennis Book Ever
The World's Best Cricket Book Ever
The World's Best Rugby Book Ever

ARNOLD SNEAD'S WORLD'S BEST GOLF BOOK EVER

. . . No wonder I'm so goddamn short; you'd be short if you had to haul 86 pounds of clubs around a golf course day after day . . .

...NTS

Foreword

Slipping on the traditional Green Jacket after winning the Masters for the first time gave me the same thrill I felt when the authors of this great book asked me to pen the foreword.

This book is a vast improvement on the hundreds of boring, tedious texts devoted to technique and style which have detracted from the excitement and emotion of this highly individual sport.

I have luckily made over 55 million dollars from golf and the many endorsements which that great lawyer Mr. Mark McCormack cleverly guided my way; my private jet whisks me from course to course. Yes, the game has been kind to me. But what is Golf?

Golf is true sport, the challenge renewed and revisited each time the ball is addressed. It is the great courses of St. Andrews, Carnoustie, Pebble Beach, Winged Foot . . . The great competitors: Jones, Snead, Nicklaus, Player, Watson, Ballesteros . . . The atmosphere, the tension, the pathos, the drama. The money.

You will never regret buying (or borrowing) this book. And remember, when looking for quality sports-wear, look for the sign of the open golf umbrella. I wear it always and look at my swing. Good luck to you all.

A. PALMER

Having sold his four iron to pay hotel bills at the Canton Hilton, Arnold Palmer attempts to repossess the weapon after the cheque for 26 Yuan bounced.

THE ABC OF GOLF

Airshot
Failing to make contact with the ball.
A complete miss like this used to be called
'missing the globe'. For reasons known only
to themselves Americans sometimes call it a
'whiff'. Airshots have been known to cause
suicides in Japan and alcoholism in Australia.

Aden
Aden became the Peoples' Republic of South
Yemen in 1968 after being a British Protecto-
rate for 129 years. Golf is still played at two
courses with 12 holes each and oiled sand
'greens'. The bunkers here are called fairways.

Allan, A. J. Travers (1875-98)
Defeated James Robb to win the British
Amateur Championship in 1897 after an
incident in which, after hooking his ball at the
11th hole, it was found in Robb's caddie's
pocket. A great shot by any standards.

Artificial Aids
Rule 37(a) prohibits the use of artificial aids or
devices which may assist in making a stroke,
measuring distance or gripping a club.
Hand-warmers are legal provided golfers use
them to warm their hands and not their balls.

Address

The rules prescribe that a golfer has addressed his ball as soon as he has taken his stance and grounded his club behind the ball. Some players continue to address the ball even after they have hit it. Talking to the ball is a degenerative complaint caused by years of frustration.

Albatross

A score of three below par for a hole. Extremely rare bird, the more common claim is to have "birdied" a hole or even "eagled" which is two below par.

Advice

Any suggestion which could influence a golfer in deciding how to play, what club to use etc. Can be sought or accepted only from a player's partner or caddy. Gratuitous advice offered by spectators can result in hazards (to the spectators).

Australian Golf Club

Formed in 1882 it boasts Sydney's premier course, 7116 yards long and re-designed in 1977 by Jack Nicklaus. Nicklaus added 3 lakes, 3 new holes and went on to set a course record of 68 in the 1978 Australian Open.

Alex 'Sandy' Herd, British Open champion 1902, in action (1923). Herd was famous for his 'waggles' before hitting the ball. Three years after this photo was taken he waggled well enough to become the British Professional Match Play champion for the second time, at the tender age of 58.

Jock McClubhead prepares to tee off at the annual clans match and beautiful knees competition.

The Alcatraz touring team at the Texas Open, 1895.

African golf cart, circa 1930

Armour, Tommy

Won the U.S. Open in 1927, beating Harry Cooper. One week later he lost 5 balls and took 23 strokes to get down at the 17th hole of the Shawnee Open.

Amateurism
In the 1981 New Zealand Open the left handed Amateur Claude Riordan holed-in-one at the 12th where the prize for professionals was a $10,000 car. To compensate the luckless Riordan and preserve his status as an amateur the tournament committee gave his wife a $147 food blender.

Ayton, David

Led the 1885 St. Andrews Open by 5 shots at the 17th. Played his second to the green and then from green to bunker, to road to bunker, and back and forth for an 11. He lost his composure and the Open by two strokes.

THE **ABC** OF GOLF

Back Door
Describes that part of the hole on the green furthest from the player putting — also termed the "Tradesman's Entrance."

Burglar
A Golfer who inflates his handicap and thereby gives himself a competitive edge in a match.

Bunker
Sand-filled pits which surround greens to prevent golfers making par. Known in U.S.A. as traps.

Birdie
A score of one below par for a hole. If a player puts his ball into rough or trees he is unlikely to achieve birdie. But in mixed foursomes a bird in the hand is worth more than a birdie.

Blaster
Originally applied to a broad-soled wedge. Also occurs frequently on courses where Mexican food is served.

Brassie
Old term for a number 2 wood. Also describes the plaque which marks the spot on the 17th hole at Royal Lytham and St. Annes from where Bobby Jones hit a 175 yard blind bunker shot into the hole to win the 1926 British Open.

Bonallack, Michael
Top British amateur golfer of the post-war years who won every major title in Britain in the 1960's. Once said of his swing, "It's more suited to shovelling coal.".

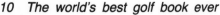

A great shot mine Fuhrer. I'd advise a three-wood from here and I'll tell the Wermacht to clear the fairway through to Poland.

Bisque

A system of handicapping in which the receiver of strokes takes them at the hole of his choice.

The term is of French origin and is also used in real tennis, croquet and by young lobsters.

Bolt, Tommy

Fearless American golfer who expressed his displeasure at the introduction of numerous petty P.G.A. rules by breaking wind loudly on the first tee. For this misdemeanour he was fined $25. Complained Tom, "Hell, they're taking all the spirit out of the game, that was an air shot — I should have only lost a stroke".

Ball, John 1861-1940

British amateur champion eight times between 1888 and 1912. Won two shillings for coming eighth in the British Open at St. Andrews when he was 15. Only ever played as an amateur after that and who can blame him.

The world's best golf book ever 11

Braid, James (1870-1950)

One of Britain's 'greats' along with Vardon and Taylor. British Open Champion in 1901, 1905, 1906, 1908, 1910. He was not a big hitter for many years until length suddenly came to him:

"It was just the same as if I went to bed a short driver one night and got up a long driver in the morning. It was . . . the greatest golfing mystery I have ever come across."

Bulger

An obsolete wooden club with a convex face. Now seen down the front of male ballet dancers' tights.

'FORE!'

Ballesteros, Severiano

Flamboyant Spaniard who won $1 million dollars in 1978 and received an award from King Juan Carlos for his contribution to Spanish sport. So grateful was he to receive this accolade that he declined to represent Spain in the 1978 World Cup as there was not enough money in it.

Buggy

Or golf cart. A battery powered conveyance which has removed any element of athleticism from American golf.

Balls

American golfers in 1980 purchased 627,846,014 golf balls. (That's a lot of balls, Ed.).

Barnes, Brian

British golfer who took 13 putts on the 8th hole (par 3) at St. Cloud. Having used up most of his strokes Barnes left the course.

Brown, Jim

American actor and former Cleveland Browns running back, convicted of a misdemeanor battery after he punched and choked his golf partner Frank Snow during a friendly match at the Western Avenue Golf Course Los Angeles. The match was lost, as was a $20 bet. Brown was sued for $250,000 damages.

THE **ABC** OF GOLF

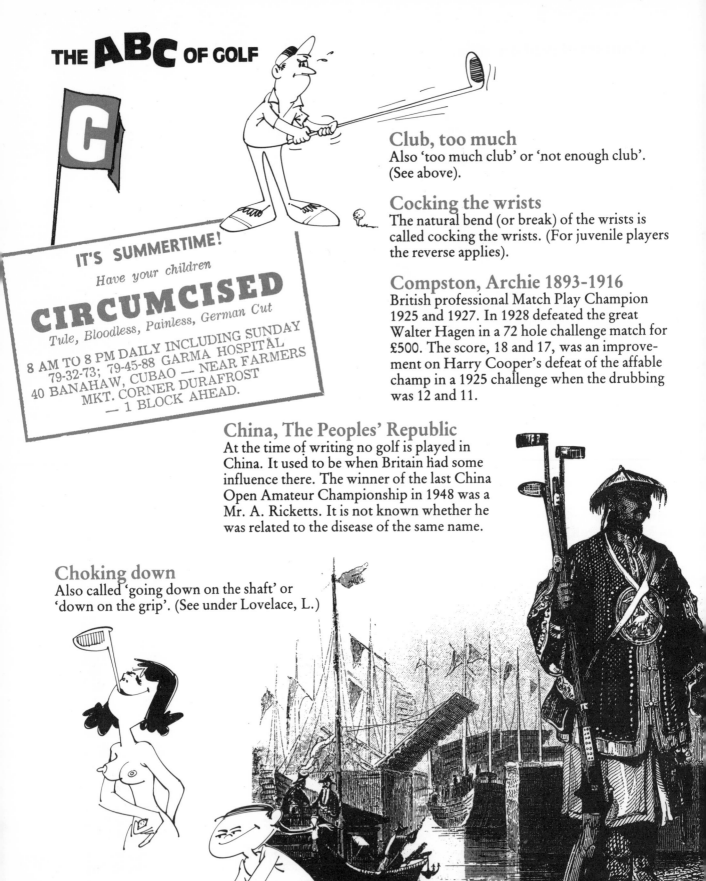

Club, too much
Also 'too much club' or 'not enough club'.
(See above).

Cocking the wrists
The natural bend (or break) of the wrists is
called cocking the wrists. (For juvenile players
the reverse applies).

Compston, Archie 1893-1916
British professional Match Play Champion
1925 and 1927. In 1928 defeated the great
Walter Hagen in a 72 hole challenge match for
£500. The score, 18 and 17, was an improvement on Harry Cooper's defeat of the affable
champ in a 1925 challenge when the drubbing
was 12 and 11.

China, The Peoples' Republic
At the time of writing no golf is played in
China. It used to be when Britain had some
influence there. The winner of the last China
Open Amateur Championship in 1948 was a
Mr. A. Ricketts. It is not known whether he
was related to the disease of the same name.

Choking down
Also called 'going down on the shaft' or
'down on the grip'. (See under Lovelace, L.)

Courses played on, most

American golfer Ralph Kennedy had played on 3,615 courses when he retired aged 71 in 1953.

If all the courses he played on were laid end to end Kennedy would probably have died of thirst.

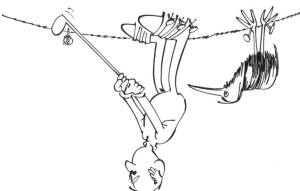

Charles, Bob

The first left-handed professional of undisputed world class. Charles is of course a right-handed player in his native New Zealand which is upside down.

Cabbage Pounder

A player who spends considerable time and energy in the rough.

Scottish foot fetishists in action at St. Andrews around the turn of the century.

Cup, Ryder
Offered by seed merchant, Samuel Ryder in 1927 as the prize in a match between American and English teams. Played for only every two years because American players get tired of lifting the cup aloft.

Cup, Walker
Another biennial event, but played by amateurs, particularly the Great Britain/Ireland side which has won only a couple of times since 1922.

Cup, Curtis
And yet another biennial fixture. Played between the ladies of Britain and the U.S., the monotonous U.S. victories since the cup's inception in 1932 strongly suggest that Great Britain was much better at ruling three-quarters of the earth's surface than pushing a ball around a small course.

Clairvoyant.
After heading the first round of the Mayne Nickless P.G.A. Tournament in Melbourne 1981 Ken Brown said "I've got no chance of winning this one". Leading after the Second round he quipped "I'm just not good enough and I'm not going in for a lot of bull by saying otherwise". Still leading after three rounds Brown predicted, "I can't win this championship . . . I'm expecting to blow up any moment". Brown was right . . . he blew to 9th position and was penalised two strokes for slow play as he zig-zagged through the final round.

Card
A document submitted by golfers at the conclusion of a round. Sometimes contains a record of all the strokes actually played.

Gary Player's caddy is overcome with tension and emotion as Player wins his 13th South African Open title, 1981.

Player and son.

Caddie
Leathery old retainer who carries clubs and gives advice as to how to play each hole. Must be able to mask all emotions including the temptation to roll on the ground with hilarity.

Caddie-boys
Last century at the Royal Hong Kong Golf Club they called the game 'Hittee-ball-say-damn'.
Many present day members still use the term.

THE **ABC** OF GOLF

Dimple
Found on the surface of golf balls.

Dimple
Whiskey consumed by the gallon in Scotland especially at St. Andrews. Most Scottish golfers are powered by it.

Dormie (Dormy)
A situation in play where a golfer or team are ahead in a match by as many holes as there are left to play and therefore unbeatable. The term originates from the French verb "dormir" as the player or team in that happy state can go to sleep and still win.

De Bendern, Count John 1907-
Born John De Forest, he won the British Amateur Championship in 1932 despite suffering, in Bernard Darwin's words, "from the waggling disease in its most aggravated form". (See 'Waggle').

Divot
Trench-like tear in the fairway made by golfers who hit the ground before the ball. Divots should be replaced unless they are too heavy to lift.

Deemed to Move
"A ball is deemed to have moved if it leaves its position and comes to rest in any other place".
(Rules of Golf and an extract from 'Golfers' Handbook of Logic".)

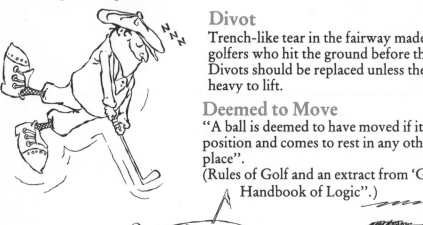

Stay in tight on 'im you guys! The Umbrella emblem alone's worth a fortune.

DEAR DOCTOR

Dear Doctor,
About 18 years ago I completed a round at the club and headed for the 19th for a few belts with the boys. After numerous drinks my feet became attached to the bar stool and I've been here ever since. What do you suggest (hic!). My wife keeps phoning because my dinner's getting cold.

> *Yours,*
> *Al Koholic c/o 4th stool from the*
main entrance to the bar,
> *Elmwood Country Club, New York.*

Try taking off your spikes. I would add that research has shown most women to be born nags. Stay where you are.

Dear Doctor,
I am writing to thank you for your advice on treating my painful lower-back which was making me slice very badly off the tee. Your suggestion that I face 90 degrees in the opposite direction to the fairway has me slicing right-up the middle every time. The pain is worse than ever but golf, as indeed life itself, was not always meant to be fun. Thanks again.

> *Yours,*
> *Vince Masochist*
> *Fort Lauderdale, Fla.*

Dear Doctor,
A few weeks ago I was washing some golf balls when one slipped out of my hands and into my mouth, whereupon I swallowed it in astonishment.

I've tried everything but nothing will shift it and I just keep swelling so much that I've gained 44 pounds in weight. What can I do? The boys at the club are mocking me unmercifully.

Try bran and prunes in the mornings and if that doesn't work, swallow a well-oiled 3 iron. That'll shift anything.

Dear Doctor,
When I crouch slightly to putt, I get the most awful stabbing pain in the back. What can I do? It doesn't happen when I drive or chip.

Well obviously you can't drive or chip your putts. So either put up with the pain or go and see a doctor.

Dear Doctor,
I lost a leg in the First War, but happily I am still able to play the Royal and Ancient Game. In fact my handicap has improved as a result. My only problem is that my stump gets very sore and tender after 72 holes or so. Is there anything I can do?
Yours,
Albert Trench, age 89
Troon, Scotland

I should not need to remind a veteran of the Great War that golf is not a game for the weak-willed, lily-livered, sissies or cowards. Go and cry on someone else's shoulder.

Dear Doctor,
I read with interest your recent feature article entitled 'Causes and Cures for Golf Elbow'. The same article by another doctor appeared a year ago in Tennis Today magazine. All you appear to have done is substitute the word 'golf' wherever the word 'tennis' appears. Surely you must offer some sort of explanation?
Yours,
Payne Hertz (Mr.)
Banana Grove Alaska

Sarcasm is the lowest form of wit. We authors are plagued by amateur critics. Try writing an article yourself sometime; you unimaginative cretin.

Dear Doctor,
Back in Australia we play an annual tournament at my club where the players must drink a double Jamaican rum at the start of each hole. It's a 36 hole event. Last year I was lucky enough to win the tournament with a score of 407. However, on the way to the 19th for a celebratory drink, I walked into a tree and broke my nose. Is it normal for top pros in the euphoria of victory to injure themselves in this way?

No doubt most of the injuries to the top players happen in this way. Of course you and I never get to see the victors after they throw their putter in the air at the final hole. I would add that our figures show that last year falling putters were responsible for more head injuries than car accidents.

THE **ABC** OF GOLF

Evans, Charles 'Chick' 1890-
U.S. Open Champion, 1916. In 1962 he played in his 50th consecutive U.S. Amateur Championship. Famous for carrying only seven clubs and sometimes as many as four putters because his putting tended to be erratic. That didn't stop his 286 total in the 1916 U.S. Open being unbeaten for 20 years.

Evans, Chick
In 1919 he had three-putted the formidable 14th green at the Oakmont Country Club and in frustration and disgust used his umbrella handle to hole out.

Teeing off at the 'Custer Classic' Mixed Pairs Championship, Little Big Horn course, May 1847.

Loosen Up On That Swing — the natural way

Top professional golfers all agree that tension is the enemy of a perfect, easy swing. Different pros teach different methods of overcoming a tense swing. We've tried most of them. But the real answer to match tension is alcohol. Drink a great deal of whisky, gin, vodka or even methylated spirits, just as long as it relaxes you and lets you play loose as nature intended.

THE ABC OF GOLF

Fairway
Mown portion of the playing area of a course between the tee and green. Weekend players normally move up this area in a sideways manner, dropping balls down their trousers as they go.

Feathery
Early golf balls were leather suffed tight with a hat full of feathers and called 'featheries'. 'Feathery' has often been used to describe the tongues of members after a lengthy session at the 19th.

Feel of a club
See under 'Hooker'.

Fade
A term used by professional golfers to describe a situation where they have hit an uncontrolled slice but want to make it look intentional.

> "It's not a very nice thing to wake up one morning and find you can't play the game anymore."
>
> *Bruce Crampton*

Fore
A word shouted by a golfer after his ball has hit another player.

THE ABC OF GOLF

G

Golf ball sales
It's estimated that about 13,000,000 are sold in the U.K. each year. In the U.S. the figure is in the region of 130,000,000. What a lot of balls!

Golf, Origin of the word
Although the Scots, Germans, Dutch, Icelanders and just about everyone else claim to have originated the word, it is now generally accepted to have originated from 'flog' spelt backwards. An ancient Serbo-Croat word meaning 'to flay the genitalia with a damp raffle ticket'.

Greensome
Said to be a type of four-ball match. Also called a 'Canadian Foursome' or 'Selective Scotch Ball' and proof positive that golf is a silly game.

Golf
The Royal and Ancient game was played by seven successive monarchs of the Stuart line and later by the Duke of Windsor and George VI. The present royals prefer horses.

Ground under Repair (G.U.R.)
Like most other hazards an area where the authors' balls inevitably wing their errant way. Balls can be removed from G.U.R. normally without penalty but usually at point of entry and no nearer the hole. (work that lot out).

ELLIMANS UNIVERSAL EMBROCATION 1/1½

"IT I WILL HAVE OR I WILL HAVE NONE"

Prepared only by Elliman Sons & Co Slough

For STIFFNESS SPRAINS — ACHES BRUISES

Gilder, Bob.
At the 1981 Glen Campbell Los Angeles Open, Tom Watson was the man to beat and Gilder said he could beat him. "I respect Watson, but he's nothing special," said Gilder. "He can be beaten. I know I can beat him. He's a great player, but I think I'm a great player also or I wouldn't be here". Watson won.

Gambling

"Amateur golf is to be played for its own sake and not for profit. When gambling motives are introduced evils can arise to threaten the integrity of both the game and individual players".
Royal and Ancient Golf Club of St. Andrews Policy.

Green

The prepared putting surface, named after American professional Hubert Green who spent a lot of time on them until he learnt to putt accurately.

GOLF and LAW

On the 7th of September 1925 at the West Runton Golf Course, a Miss Jeanie Cameron Cleghorn was hit in the face by a golf club wielded in a practice swing by Miss Cicely Mary Oldham. Miss Oldham was swinging at an imaginary ball, followed through and knocked the unfortunate Miss Cleghorn unconscious.

Seeking compensation and damages Miss Cleghorn's case was heard by a judicial golfer, Mr. Justice Swift who, having heard evidence that Miss Oldham spoke to an imaginary ball then struck at it, observed "You do not speak to the ball before you drive; you speak to it *after* you drive. "Addressing a jury is one thing, addressing a ball is another" the learned Judge ruled.

In awarding the injured plaintiff £150, Mr. Justice Swift stated it was without foundation to argue that spectators enjoyed golf all the more because they may be struck by ball or club "The language one hears in that event does not suggest the experience is pleasurable". This was held to be a case where no risk had been assumed or undertaken and the damages were properly awarded.

Lord Justice Sellers in 1962 heard a similar case of a hapless golfer who struck his ball from deep rough when his companions, at his invitation, had walked ahead. His cry of "fore" as the ball sped on its way ensured that one of the players turned and was struck in the eye. "The player's actions were not only negligent but demonstrated a total disregard for the safety of those he knew were in the line of danger and damages must follow the event."

NB. No reported case has been found arising from President Gerald Ford hitting a spectator in a Pro.-Am tournament in 1976.

"The only consistent thing in golf is its inconsistency."
Jack Nicklaus

Aussie pro star Jan Stephenson was arrested by Atlanta police shortly after this photo was taken. The Aussie pro star had attempted to steal a dozen balls from the LPGA tournament by stuffing them up her shirt.

Golf — "The Dangerous Game"

New York — P.A. — 21 September, 1966 NY TIMES

It may come as surprise to the non-golfer, but the ancient Scottish pastime in its modern guise is becoming one of the world's most dangerous sports.

Each weekend players are being carried off golf courses with broken bones, crushed ribs, fractured ankles and assorted injuries usually associated with such contact sports as grid-iron football and ice hockey.

The game of golf is as harmless as ever, barring a shanked drive which hits someone on the adjoining fairway.

The trouble is the motorised golf cart, a vehicle which has become mandatory on most American courses and which the National Safety Council warns has become "a safety problem that warrants immediate attention."

Golfers riding in golf carts are crashing into each other, falling off bridges, toppling over on hillsides and submerging in lakes and other water hazards.

Golf course operators blame the drivers, alleging that older golfers get into trouble because of slow reflexes and faulty eyesight, and the younger ones often go out for a round drunk.

"Liquor is our nemesis," said one Mid-West golf club director. He said members of a local civic club got so drunk during lunch that they played a game of "chicken" with their carts during the afternoon round, deliberately ramming each other head on.

"No one was injured," he said, "but they were feeling no pain anyway."

In 1980 Guy Wolstenholme won the Victorian Open, holding off challenges from Ben Crenshaw and Graham Marsh. It was the English professional's fourth victory in the event. Said an apprehensive Mrs Wolstenholme "Every time he wins the Victorian Open I get pregnant"

A tough one David ...I think the borrow goes left

Who let him off a Tennis Court.

"The unimaginative clot with a sound method can make a good golfer, but it takes brains to make a great one."
Peter Dobereiner

IN MEMORIUM
"Here he lies God rest his soul
Lies at rest by the 19th hole
Poetic justice you may say
He always lied there anyway."

"The hardest golf shot is a mashie struck 90 yards from the green where the ball is played against an oak tree, bounced into a sandtrap, skipped off a stone, run onto the green and then rolls into the cup. This shot is so difficult I have only played it once."
Zeppo Marx

THE **ABC** OF GOLF

Harrogate Open

At this event in 1926 one A. H. Evans concluding his round at the 18th Green by sinking a 20 yard putt threw his putter into the air in excitement. Unfortunately for his partner, Mr. F. J. Crankshaw, the club landed on his head rendering him unconscious.

Hollywood Handicap

Having an overweight, old or mildly unsuccessful friend in Los Angeles. Can also refer to an unrealistic handicap that makes you sound like a star player.

Hooding the club

(See 'Family Planning for Young Marrieds'. We don't print that sort of filth and innuendo.)

Hungary

Used to have an Amateur Open Championship going back to 1902, but what with World War II, annexation by Russia and a crushed uprising, you would have to have a death-wish to be seen with golf clubs in Budapest these days.

Handicap

A golfer's partner.

Heather Hutchinson

Used a 3-iron to despatch a seven-foot kangaroo which attacked her on Wylcatchem golf club Western Australia. The 'roo was stunned. Pundits say the club selection was all wrong and a driver should have been used.

Hernia
Undescended ball.

Hospital Zone
Practice tee and fairway.

Hitler, Adolf
German No. 1 between 1939 and 1945. Played with only one ball, last seen in a bunker in Berlin looking very Braunned off.

BIG BIRDIE

Police said yesterday that they have charged a young Moroccan man in Syros, Greece, with sexually assaulting a pelican, the mascot of the neighbouring Island of Tinos. The pelican died from internal haemorrhage, police said.

They said that a trial was suspended yesterday when the Moroccan asked for legal representation and will be continued today. The man, identified as Abdel Brim Talal, aged 28, was arrested on Saturday in Tinos when traces of blood and feathers were found on his clothes.

The pelican, Marcos, was one of two males on the island, much beloved by the locals. He was found wounded late on Friday in a public toilet, and a veterinarian's examination showed that he had been sexually assaulted. The bird died shortly afterwards.

Police said that a group of enraged islanders attacked the suspect. He was saved by police intervention. Press reports said that two German tourists had also filed complaints against Talal for attempted rape, but police did not confirm this.

The press also reported that the body of the pelican will be stuffed and kept on Tinos.—AP.

August 11, 81 The Guardian-London & Manchester

Honour
What the Royal and Ancient Club at St. Andrews accorded Hagen, Locke and Cotten in 1968 by granting these foreigners honorary membership.

Honour
The privilege of playing first off a tee this is indicated by the term "your Honour". Not to be confused with the obsequious term used by prisoners when addressing a judge about to sentence them.

Hook
Opposite to slice. Occurs when the ball is hit in an uncontrolled manner from right to left. Golfers who habitually execute shots in this way are not all necessarily hookers.

Hagen-Walter
Former caddy from Rochester New York who earned a million dollars and dominated world golf in the 1920's. Beat Bobby Jones 11 and 10 in a 72 hole match in 1927.

Hogan, William Benjamin
Another former caddy who between 1946 and 1953 won the U.S. Open four times, the Masters twice the American PGA twice and the British Open once, also a Grand Slam in 1953.

Hole
18 of these are spread around a golf course cunningly protected by vast stretches of water, tall trees, rough grass and bunkers. Golf balls are seldom attracted to them.

Finalists in the English 'Lovely Cap Competition', 1904.

Diminutive English comedian, Ronnie Corbett, one of golf's most powerful putters, pictured shortly before teeing off. He fell into a divot near the 17th hole and was lost for two days.

About the Authors

Muirfield, St. Andrews, Royal Lytham St. Anne's, Winged Foot, Pebble Beach and Augusta National, Sherwood and Alderdice are familiar with them all.

"The Royal and Ancient Course has particular memories for me," Alderdice recalls. "I was playing with myself (he usually went around on his own) the very same day after the Open had finished when I tripped over a bloody great brass plaque, sticking out of the ground at the 10th hole, which said something about a man called Jones. Well, I don't have to tell you I nearly broke my neck. So I came back late that night, dug the thing out and buried it under the 17th green to make certain nobody else hurt themselves."

Sherwood, an Australian golfing journalist, is mostly remembered for his 28 page essay in Golfing Today (Aug 1959), entitled "Why Nicklaus Will Never Make It As Top Pro".

A full pipe band, a three minute drum roll and he still hooks his drive out of bounds.

The Prince of Wales, 1923.

40

THE **ABC** OF GOLF

Irons
What you hang your partner from when he misses a 10" putt on the 18th green to lose the match.

'Take no notice of them. Just relax and play your natural game'.

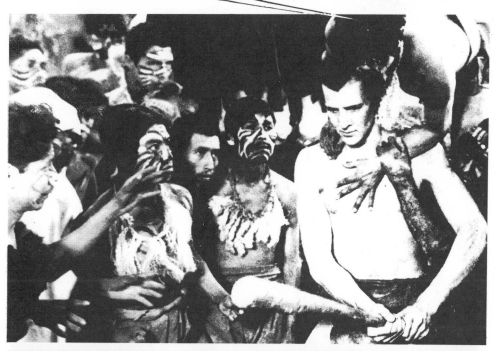

Iranian touring pro, Muhammed Aziz, officiates at public clubbing of his wife after finding her in bed with a pork chop.

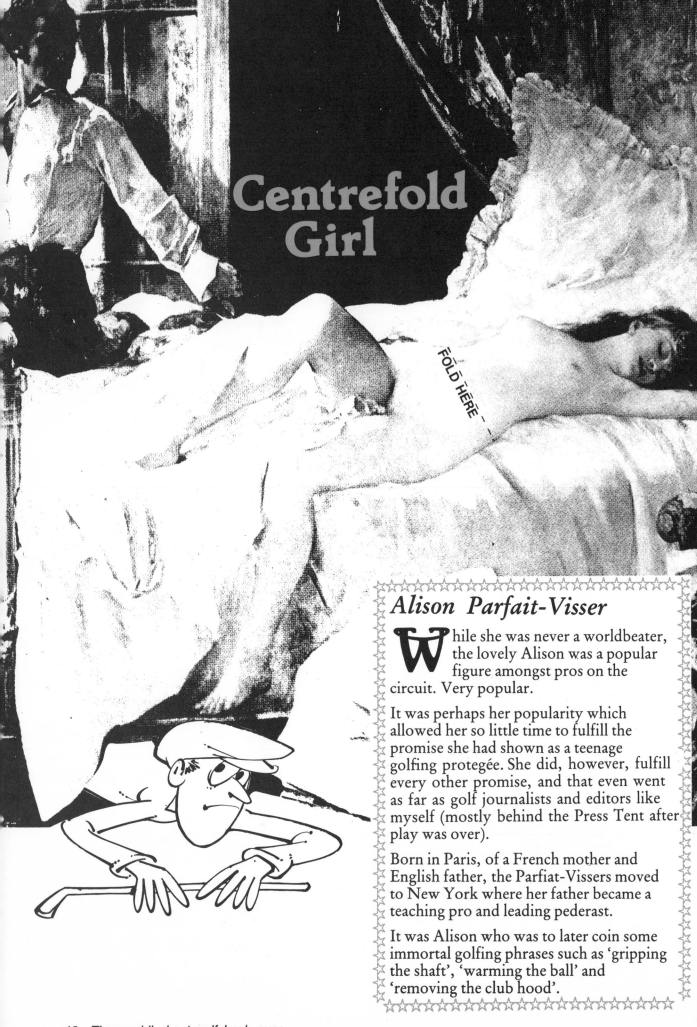

Centrefold Girl

FOLD HERE

☆ *Alison Parfait-Visser* ☆

While she was never a worldbeater, the lovely Alison was a popular figure amongst pros on the circuit. Very popular.

It was perhaps her popularity which allowed her so little time to fulfill the promise she had shown as a teenage golfing protegée. She did, however, fulfill every other promise, and that even went as far as golf journalists and editors like myself (mostly behind the Press Tent after play was over).

Born in Paris, of a French mother and English father, the Parfiat-Vissers moved to New York where her father became a teaching pro and leading pederast.

It was Alison who was to later coin some immortal golfing phrases such as 'gripping the shaft', 'warming the ball' and 'removing the club hood'.

THE ABC OF GOLF

Jacklin, Tony O.B.E.

Former Scunthorpe caddy who won the British Open in 1969 and the U.S. Open in 1970. Faded and had his U.S. Tournament card forfeited in 1974.

Jones, Bobby

A Harvard graduate in Law, Science and Technology who also found time to become the World's Best Golfer Ever. He won 4 U.S. Opens, 5 U.S. Amateurs, and 3 British Opens. The Scots awarded him the freedom of St. Andrews in 1927. So touched was he that he retired in 1933 and returned to his law practice.

James, Mark

English professional who was called before a Zambian Golf Committee in 1978 after hurling his putter into a tree. Asked if he had deliberately thrown it there he replied, "No, it was entirely accidental, I was trying to throw it into a pond.".

"A golf course is the epitome of all that is purely transitory in the universe, a space not to dwell in but to get over as quickly as possible"

— *Jean Giraudoux 1933*

"Unlike the other Scottish game of whisky drinking, excess in Golf is not injurious to the health."

Sir Walter Simpson

POLYNESIE FRANÇAISE

POSTES

16F

GOLF D'ATIMAONO

RF

THE **ABC** OF GOLF

Kolbe
The German claim. (See under Golf, Origin of the word.)

Kolf
The Dutch claim. (See under Word, Origin of the golf.)

Kuramoto
Masahira, Japanese golfer banned from representing his country in the World Cup after a marijuana bust. Had apparently read that golfers should try to stay on the grass.

"HUBBY'S love for GOLF leads to divorce"

Arkansas Gazette 12th March 1982

Shapely Dolores Richards, 46, was given a divorce because of her husband's unreasonable behaviour, reports from La Jolla California claim.

He has a love affair with a demanding mistress ... golf.

Mrs Richards named the exclusive La Jolla Golf and Country Club for alienating her husband's affections in her testimony on Tuesday for a divorce decree at San Diego County Court.

She claimed that her husband scored more often on the course than in the matrimonial bed. He could instantly recall golf statistics but forgot her birthday.

When the couple separated two months ago Mr. Richards astonished his wife by going to live in the Golf Club pavillion sleeping in the locker room while waiting for their case to be heard.

Mr. Richards, 53, retired, did not contest his wife's petition and did not attend court ... he was touring with the Golf Club to Ensenada 86 miles away.

When our reporter told him of the court decision ending his 27 year marriage he said: "I don't blame Dolores, I told her from the very beginning that golf came first, but she didn't believe me".

A club member said "Chuck will be welcomed by the other 28 divorcees in the Club who have all been victims of marital intolerance. All we want to do is play golf, have a good time and be happy".

"I'm stumped when it comes to pick the hardest shot in golf for me, but I know the easiest one . . . the first shot at the 19th hole."

— W. C. Fields 1925

Happy Bells hit the right note

London, Aug 20.
Janet Bell (25), who is training to be an opera singer, swung her No 2 wood and holed in one over the 253 yards of the 18th tee at Sidmouth Golf Club, Devon.

Then her brother Alastair (19) a trainee solicitor, stepped up with his driver and repeated the feat over the full 291-yard distance from the back tee.

He said yesterday: "It was a blind hole and when we reached the green we thought we had both gone into the rough. But as I walked past the hole I was astounded to see both balls lying in it."

Brother and sister had another bit of luck.

There were only three people in the clubhouse when they bought the traditional round of drinks for everyone present.
— AP.

THE **ABC** OF GOLF

Lady Golfer, first
Believed to be Mary, Queen of Scots who was seen to play golf just a few days after the murder of her husband in 1567. Well, how else does a widowed Queen take her mind off things?

Little, W. Lawson 1910-1968
The only man to win the American and British Amateur Championships in the same year — twice running. In 1934 he carried no fewer than 23 clubs in his bag (or rather, his hernia-prone caddy did.)

Leather Mashie
A facetious and ancient term indicating that a player or caddie has used his shoe to improve the lie of his ball. It is not known if such a term exists for the act today.

Leith Links
Old Edinburgh's golf course. Charles I was playing there in 1842 when news reached him of the rebellion in Ireland, causing him to miss a ten inch putt. As history shows, the Irish suffered awfully for interrupting his game.

Locke, Bobby
Won 44 major tournaments in 22 years, including 4 British Opens. "Old Muffin Face" plundered the U.S. golfing coffers with style. He slept with his rusty putter for safekeeping.

Lie
A golfer's scorecard or any statement about his handicap.

GREAT PLAYERS OF YESTERYEAR

Owen McFrigg 1874-

From 1900 to 1908 Owen 'Big O' McFrigg won the Annual West of Scotland Open Championship eleven times, a feat which may never be duplicated. Many a comparison has been drawn with this incredible record, including Bobby Jones' 'big four' in one year, Bob Beamon's thirty foot leap at the Mexico Olympics, Bjorn Borg's five straight Wimbledon titles and Martin Bormann's lucky escape from a Berlin bunker. But these feats, great though they may be, pale to insignificance alongside McFrigg's remarkable performance.

It is perhaps even more amazing as this great Scot didn't pick up a golf club until he was 36 years of age.

According to Irish records McFrigg retired from the golfing scene shortly before his fortieth birthday. McFrigg is presently believed to be either in suburban Glasgow, or dead, which is preferable.

Grim Scottish police escort American Bobby Jones from the course after he had stolen the 1927 British Open. A golfing recidivist Jones won the Grand Slam in 1930.

Menu. Today's Special:
Boiled tripe and cabbage.

Lema, Tony

Flamboyant American Golfer "Champagne Tony" had Gary Player on the ropes in 1965 leading by 7 holes with 17 to play then by 5 holes with 9 to play in the Piccadilly World Match Play Championship at Wentworth. Player won. It was later said of the unfortunate Lema that "he had wrung one more spectacular defeat from the jaws of victory".

Lost Ball

A ball is declared to be lost if it is not found within five minutes, or is abandoned. This would seem to make good sense.

Laidlay, John E. born 1860

British Amateur Champion, 1889. Was said to have been the first man to play golf in Egypt, which is akin to claiming to be the first Chilean to visit Alice Springs.

Letters to the Editor

Dear Sir,
The Royal and Ancient game as played in the United Kingdom traditionally involves the use of the so called "small ball", whereas American golfers swear by the "big ball". In reality there is 1/16th of an inch variation in circumference.

This insignificant difference has led to volumes of debate as to which ball has the better qualities.

Critics of the small ball opine that it is succeptible to fade or draw, they applaud the big ball for its aerodynamic advantage.

What I want to ask you is — does the size of a ball have any relationship to length and what about the 4½ inch hole circumference? Is it proposed to have bigger holes to accommodate big balls?
Yours ever,
Reggie R. Slick
c/o the large bunker near the 9th hole Carnoustie.

Dear Reggie,
Ball size has no meaningful relationship to length. It all depends on the stroke and swing, when you cock your wrists and bring the hip through. Why don't you write to us about your game next time.

Ed.

Dear Sir,
I have followed Jack Nicklaus around all the big courses, Troon, St. Andrews, Pebble Beach and Marion and have noticed his unique distinctive style which, particularly on the drive, involves a waggling of the club head and a slight forward pressure before the backswing begins.

The swing itself is hardly a thing of beauty and cannot be compared with the impeccable style of the great Bobby Jones.
Jack Spoon.
c/o Wounded Knee Post Office,
Utah.

Dear Jack,
When you can earn a million dollars a year and drive 300 yards up the middle, we'll listen to you.

Ed.

Dear Sir,
I decided to take up golf last week. I bought a Gary Player cap, an Arnold Palmer Shirt, Sammy Snead shoes, a full matched set of Tom Kite Clubs and some balls endorsed by Nancy Lopez. On the first tee I settled in, wiggling my hips to such a degree that a lady waiting in a mixed foursome fainted dead away. My first golf shot drove a new Dunlop 65 unerringly over the fence to my right, onto a four-lane highway. It smashed through the windscreen of an oncoming semi-trailer which hit six cars. I have received fifteen writs — what should I do?
"Novice"
co/ Winged Foot Golf Club New York

Dear Novice,
From the sound of things you have bad slice — bring your right hand over a bit further on the shaft.

Ed.

Great Feats in Golf —

Dr. Livingstone in Africa

Livingstone with head caddie Obelisk Freeman at the start of the epic record attempt.

On a December morning in 1840, Doctor David Livingstone set out from the port of Liverpool for Africa on what would mistakenly become known as one of the world's great feats of exploration and endurance.

Eight years later the world would hear of the disappearance of Livingstone and later of the triumphant meeting of Livingstone and Henry Moreton Stanley in the steaming jungle hinterland.

Only recently did the world learn of Livingstone's massive cover-up: on the pretext of exploration David Livingstone had attempted to play golf from one side of Africa to the other in under 3,000,000 strokes, which was considered to be par at the time.

On his arrival in Capetown the tireless Scot recruited 420 bearers to carry food, equipment and the more than 20,000 new balls required for the epic attempt. Twenty-six horses were loaded up with 600 sets of clubs, 1,000 pairs of spikes, 1,200 pairs gloves and a dozen caddies.

On 26 April 1843, Dr. David Livingstone teed off outside the Army barracks mess. hut in Mombasa, driving 180 yards with a 2 wood across the main road and knocking a passing policeman clear off his ostrich. He nervously sliced his second shot into the trees and, followed by his expedition,was swallowed up by the African jungle. Three months later Livingstone had flailed and slashed his way west to the shores of Lake Victoria, a formidable water hazard by any standards. After consultation with his head caddy Livingstone agreed that the 120 mile-wide lake was too wide to drive so he set off with 3-iron, chipping around its soggy shores to the Limpopo river. At this stage the Missionary's score card totalled 986,224.

Stanley presents Livingstone with the dreaded lunch bill.

Swamp. For miles nothing but swamp and wasteland. It was the biggest water-logged sand trap he'd ever seen. Livingstone was in dire trouble. More than half his men were dead. Worse, the handle of his favorite sandwedge snapped when beating off a crocodile attack.

Still he pressed on to discover the Victoria Falls where, after losing 954 balls he was to crack his best drive of the expedition 310 yards, only to have his ball eaten by a large baboon on the other side.

It cost him a penalty stroke. Livingstone wept. Emaciated and mentally exhausted he pushed on. It was all irons now; wood shots being for the most part impossible to play in the often impenetrable undergrowth.

Not that it mattered: termites had eaten most of the clubs plus the heads off two of his best caddies. He played on, through stampeding elephants and chipping high over packs of feeding lions and hyena. By now he was low on balls; something nobody though would ever happen to the courageous doctor.

On the dry, hard plains he putted relentlessly from waterhole to waterhole, producing shots averaging 65′ and further in the choking dust.

By the time he reached half way he had passed 2,000,000 strokes. Fourteen half-literate bearers, hand-picked to complete the score cards, had gone mad and were put down. Two million shots and the wretched Livingstone was still

Livingstone's remaining caddies at practice.

time to the distant jungle drums, while thousands of miles away his wife waited. But the mosquitoes were the worst; they were huge and attacked in their thousands, which was unusual for Edinburgh in February. His wife never complained, keeping in close touch with the life assurance company and with Dunlops who had secretly sponsored the venture.

By morning the remnants of the expedition had run off into the bush and disappeared. The great explorer was lost and alone. Cursing loudly he put on his last pair of spikes and stubbornly teed off, slicing his ball into a pack of startled gnus drinking at a waterhole. This was the shot of a man not blessed with life's good timing. There wasn't another water hole for 150 miles around and the luckless Livingstone had landed right in the middle of it.

It was ten years since the good doctor had left Scotland. Family and friends had given him up for dead.

A writ was issued by his golf club in Edinburgh for an overdue bar bill and his wife was negotiating with the Daily Express over the rights to "Livingstone's Battle with Agrophobia".

By now the obsessed Scotsman was chipping mechanically and hitting has 2 and 3 irons with little length and even less purpose. He had no idea where he was. During one sunny September day he rudely played through a ladies foursome at the Kampala Country Club without so much as a nod. Stopping for a snack at the Clubhouse, he walked out without paying and was later pursued by the manager; the man who was eventually to find him to hand him the bill: Henry Moreton Stanley.

It was to take the incredibly mean Stanley two years of searching to present the lunch bill of two shillings and four pence to the now mad Scottish doctor. It was more than the dour Livingstone could endure. Flinging his sand wedge into the nearby source of the Nile, he fell backwards into a bunker screaming, "I didn't order chips. I'll pay you the two shillings, but I didn't order fourpence worth of chips!"

unable to control the dreadful slice which had gotten worse as he weakened. It was the slice which was to be Livingstone's undoing, sending him in a long semi-circle and back towards base. On the 4th of June 1848, Dr. David Livingstone played his last shot of the day from the innards of a dead rhino, then collapsed, exhausted and angry with himself for taking three strokes to extricate his ball from the bloody and flyblown hazard.

"God!", he screamed. "Dear, dear God! In the name of Jesus help me! Please, please help me." It was too late. Nobody was there to assist him or to tell him that he was breaking his wrists too early on the shot and lifting his head slightly before he struck the ball. His awful slice would only get worse. Frustrated and worn out he shot a couple of bearers to relieve the terrible tension, drank a bottle of Dimple and went to bed with Sam Snead's "Golf, My Way".

During the day the heat was relentless. At night by the lamplight in his tent, Livingstone would practice his swing, trying everything he'd ever read in a frantic effort to correct the slice which had plagued him from the very beginning. His native bearers would watch in awe as the doctor's shadow on the tent wall moved in

Bob Hope and Arnold Palmer in Africa during Hope's attempt to beat Livingstone's trans-Africa record.

Morris

'Old Tom' won four of the first eight British Open Championships at Prestwick, his home course. Once the venue was changed he never won again. His son, 'Young Tom' Morris won the title for three successive years until he died aged 32.

The great British professional 'Old Tom' Morris is seen here doing his George Bernard Shaw impersonation.

◁ Young Tom & Old Tom Morris

Mosely, John

On 7th July 1972 John Mosely having paid Green fees was about to commence a morning round of golf at the Delaware Park Golf Club, Buffalo, New York when he was challenged on the tee by an armed security guard over whether or not the Green fee had been paid. A scuffle developed, a shot was fired, and Mosely, struck in the chest, died on the way to hospital. His wife was awarded $131,250 damages and the guard received 7½ years imprisonment for second degree manslaughter.

Moonball

The only recorded shot was hit by Alan B. Shepard an American astronaut who drove a golf ball 926 yards on the Moon on the 5th of February 1971. His first attempt was a 'SPACESHOT'.

Messieux, Samuel 1793-1859

A Swiss who, for reasons best known to himself, moved to Dundee where he became an excellent golfer. He once drove a 'feathery' from the 14th tee at St. Andrews, a distance of about 380 yards. Had Msr. Messieux been using today's equipment and a modern ball the shot might still be travelling.

Merry

When the ball runs yards past the hole, as in "that putt was a bit merry". Also said to be 'steamy'. Players who consistently hit these shots are seldom merry but often the latter.

'Leaping' Lee Elder auditioning for the 1974 Minstrels Show.

Meissner, Richard. E.

American professional golfer who won nothing at all in the 1977-78 P.G.A. season. Police in Virginia and Maryland discovered he had robbed 19 banks of over $100,000 which earnt him a handicap of 25 years.

Mulligan

Practice named after Irish amateur J. B. "Hacker" Mulligan who invariably hit his first tee-shot out of bounds. This shot was treated as a warm-up or "sighter" and Mulligan would calmly play a second teeshot without penalty.

Mixed Foursome

Often called a 'gruesome' or a 'quarrelsome' and hardly ever found on courses around San Francisco.

Joe 'the Mechanic' Gambrioni — Italian born Chicago based touring pro who plays out of the Cosa Nostra Club. He has featured in 67 sudden-death playoffs and never lost one.

Make a four

(Couples in suburban California know more about this sort of thing than we do.)

Moore, T. J.

In the Dryden International Golf Tournament held at Port Arthur, Texas, Moore took a 46 at the 381 yard 18th hole hitting 20 balls into a water hazard.

The ancient Scottish elephant bird flies over the St. Andrews Course as J. F. Neville is about to play a shot. 1923.

THE **ABC** OF GOLF

Nap

A term used to describe the surface of a green and the grain direction. On a 'nappy' green one putts either with the nap (or grain), against the nap or across the nap . . . (This is madness! Ed.)

New Grampians Inn

Victorian golf course where local rules prescribe a one shot penalty for hitting a passing kangaroo.

Nichols, Bernard

In 1903 he designed and constructed the American Inverness Club nine-hole course, but built only eight holes. The committee removed a fold from the plan and he built the ninth.

> **I don't know, you pay $100 for a Golden Bear shirt and it creases all over the place.**

Nagle, Kel

Veteran Australian who, after a disastrous 82 in the 1979 New Zealand Open lowered the clubhouse flag to halfmast and declared "That is in memory of my putter which just died.".

> "95% of the putts you leave short don't go in the hole"
>
> — *Hubert Green*

"You're never beaten till you're buried —
I'm like a fine wine, I get better with age."
— Gary Player

"Golf is not agriculture".
—*Horace Hutchinson in his "Hints on Golf".*
(1866)

THE **ABC** OF GOLF

Over-40 finger

A putting technique attributed to Gene Sarazen and believed to have been used more than once for activities outside of golf.

'Your'e right, this is one hell of a sandtrap'.

One-eyed

Tommy Armour was thanks to World War 1, but went on to win every major golf championship. Retired to forge a formidable reputation as a teacher. Taught Richard Nixon but never bragged about it.

Ohio

In 1974 the State of Ohio introduced a statute making it an offence to cheat at golf.
This crime was made punishable on a second offence by a prison sentence of up to 5 years.

Old Pawky

The name given by Willie Park, Jun. to his favourite putter. It now hangs in the clubhouse of the Woking Club, Surrey, England. Inscribed on the putter are Park's own words: "It holed many a guid putt". The inscription has since been translated into English.

One-ball twosome

Eva Braun and Adolf Hitler in a bunker.

WINNING GOLF
THE 'WEASEL' WAY

For 26 years Palm Springs golfer Tom Weasel played his way profitably around the clubs of America.

He was an expert in the use of the leather Mashie, improving a thousand bad lies with his boot without detection. He finessed the act of winning in club golf to a degree not attained before or since.

Here are his ploys, culled from a career of grafting and cheating. Now, you too can make your opponent beat himself at the Royal and Ancient Game . . .

(1)   On the first tee in front of the Clubhouse make theatrical requests for silence as he prepares to drive to ensure that he is closely observed by all and that he knows it.

(2)   Even if he gets that first tense shot away remember that well timed blasts of flatulence will disrupt even Arnold Palmer's rhythm if delivered in the middle of a downswing.

(3) Point out faults in his swing or grip and watch as he flails stiffly in the direction of the ball trying to do 32 things correctly in the .08 of a second it takes to swing a club. Once he starts spraying his Dunlops into the trees tell him to relax and play his natural game.

(4) On each tee "replay" the previous hole under the pretext of checking the score: "You shanked your drive, then two in the rough, dropped out for one, a superb 4 wood into the bunker, out for 3 more, then two putts." That dreadful hole will flash before his very soul — then let him try to drive.

(5) Always carry loose change in your pocket and absently jingle it as he lines up his shot. Whistle tunelessly through your teeth. If he stares pointedly apologise profusely and keep on about the thoughtlessness of impairing his concentration.

(6) On the easiest par 3 on the course, casually remark that Gary Player once took a 6 to get down. It matters not that Player has not been within 50 miles of the course as long as your opponent thinks he has.

(7) Missing clubs are a distraction. "Lose" one of his in a bunker. Then as you walk off the green two holes on, remember where you saw it. The energy he expends rushing back under the contemptuous glares of the following foursome is good for two shots at least.

(8) On the way to any elevated tee or green, wheeze and pant up the hill. Before he tees off or plays that crucial putt, show him a small tin and ask him if he would mind putting one of the tablets under your tongue "if anything should happen". In extreme cases, should he "actually be leading", fall backwards into a bunker as he prepares to putt and lie absolutely still. He will never recover.

(9) Always point out hazards on any hole. "Water to the left, deep rough about 200 yards out." He will start to see each fair-way as a 10 foot tunnel surrounded by tiger country.

(10) When he eventually reaches the green on long putts, put your foot over the hole and hold the pin about two feet from it for him to line up on. Concede all putts on the first nine under four feet. On the second nine make him putt everything.

(11) He will eventually crack and if you observe him carefully you will notice the signs. Throbbing veins in the temples, grinding teeth, smashing clubs against trees and throwing bag and caddy into a water hazard are typical symptoms. Collect the money and always offer a return match. You will never see him again.

And remember Tom Weasel's credo . . . . "The most important thing is not to win but to take part, just as the most important thing in life is not the triumph but the struggle, the essential thing is to have fought well . . . . ."

Partner

There is an old golf saying that "one should always assume that one's partner is doing his best — until one has direct evidence to the contrary".

Pick-up hole

Where a player has a good chance of picking up a birdie. (See also 'Bachelors' Guide to Hong Kong'.)

Poland, golf in

Like almost everything else, golf failed to survive the Second World War and the subsequent Russian occupation. There has been talk of the game returning to Poland. However Solidarity want the number of holes reduced from 18 to 12.

Pitch

A high floating shot normally played to the green. Also describes the colour of Gary Player's Caddie. Is prefixed by "son-of-a" when used in America.

Plus-fours

Golf trousers quaintly but cunningly designed by Scottish players to prevent a replacement ball being dropped through a hole in the pocket, down the trouser leg and thence to the ground.

Pro-Ams

Matches which Professionals begrudgingly play with hackers on Club committees to ensure they are invited back for next year's tournament.

Palmer, Arnold

1960's Athlete of the decade who was followed by his Army of spectators whilst dominating world golf for 15 years. In 1964 he climbed 25 feet up a red gum tree at the Victoria Golf Club's 9th hole to play a shot rather than incur a penalty stroke during the Wills Masters.

Jack Nicklaus 5 time USPGA champion consoles Arnold Palmer who never won it.

Arnold Palmer, who used to think cricket was a large insect.

Mexican/American pro Lee Trevino who suffers from an acute iron deficiency.

Penalty

Penalty after carding a 66 at the Royal Melbourne Golf Club during the 1974 Chrysler Classic Lee Travino criticised the quality of the greens. "They are the biggest joke since Watergate" slammed Supermex.

An outraged Australian P.G.A. fined Trevino $500 for the comment — What do professional golfers know about greens anyway?? They're only in it for the money.

Pneumatic Balls

Sold in 1905 in Britain and America. Alex Smith won the 1905 U.S. Open Championship using one. They travelled a long way but burst easily. Smith abandoned them when two exploded in his pocket leaving him ball-less.

'It's all right for you slashing around in the rough with a bloody 2 iron . . . Who's going to buy me a new monkey?!?...

Putter

Club used to propel balls on the green into the hole. The Bulls Tool Shop of 4th Avenue Minneapolis Minnesota offers a tumescent bulls reproductive organ reinforced with steel fashioned into a putter for only $79.50 (this is not a lot of bull, Ed.).

Colonel Gaddafi's death squad in heavy disguise at the U.S. Open 1981.

THE **ABC** OF GOLF

Quail high

A shot that is deliberately played low — as high as the flight of a quail. The term was coined by Ben Hogan. Shots of this nature were often shot down by hillbillies in Hogan's native Texas.

Quicksand

What D. J. Bayley MacArthur stepped into right up to his armpits when attempting to play out of a bunker on 11th July 1931 at Rose Bay, Sydney, Australia.

Quick, Smiley Lyman 1907-

U.S. Public Links Champion 1946. No one knows why he was nicknamed Smiley but he liked it so much that he adopted it as his first name.

Gerald Ford at the 1981 Bob Hope British Classic.

THE **ABC** OF GOLF

Rabbit
Describes an indifferent golfer or a prolific sire.

Ray, Edward 'Ted' 1877-1945
A 'great' of British golf who often played in a heavy suit and with a pipe clenched between his teeth. He was a great iron player and once said, "The golfer who has not a friendly feeling for his irons is no gentleman." Who could possibly disagree with that?

Russian golf
You must be kidding, although the official Russian newspaper, Pravda, once reported that golf was 'a game which the Caucasian shepherds played with enthusiasm about 1,000 years ago'.
The Russians also invented football, tiddlywinks, baseball and ice hockey.

Royal golfers
The first were probably the later Stuart kings of Scotland. Until the 16th century the game had been banned in Acts of Scottish Parliament, although in the Accounts of the Lords High Treasurers of Scotland there are recorded payments made between 1503 and 1506 for 'Golf Clubbis and Ballis to the King that he playit with'. Sneaky old sod.

Roy, Rudolf
On the 22nd July 1971 the unfortunate Mr. Roy aged 41 was playing golf at the Montreal Country Club when, playing a difficult shot obstructed by large trees, his club shaft struck the trunk of a tree, snapped and pierced his torso, killing him.

Robertson, Allan 1815-59
The greatest golfer of his day, Robertson was born, and died, at St. Andrews. He was the first player to break 80 on the old course and to do so used a set of clubs that might have been designed in the 5th century BC. The course was far rougher than it is today and Robertson made it in 79.

Rules

There are 41 basic rules which regulate in subsections almost every conceivable situation in golf. Rules are clear unambiguous and require only the application of common sense to interpret, e.g. Rule 37(1)(i) when any part of a player's ball overhangs the hole the player must determine whether or not it is at rest — if the ball does not fall into the hole it is deemed to be at rest. Quite simple really.

Reid, John. G.

Played the first recorded golf match in America on 22nd February 1888 in a cow paddock at Yonkers Westchester County New York. When his ball came to rest in a pile of cow dung he played a shot and was penalised two strokes for striking a ball in motion.

THE **ABC** OF GOLF

Sand-wedge
A club used to try to hoist a golfer's ball out of sand. Most golfers in that situation would prefer to use a shovel or to kick the ball out when their opponent isn't looking.

Schweizer, Hans 1913-
One of Switzerland's leading amateurs and no relation to Dr. Albert who spelt his name with a 't' and played the organ.

Stewart, Rufus
Professional at South Australia's famed Kooyonga course, who, in 1931, scored a 77 playing the course at night, using only one ball and assisted by a friend holding a kerosene lamp.

Simplex
A type of centre-shafted putter on the market around 1905. When the famous St. Andrews professional, Andrew Kirkaldy was shown a Simplex he said, "I wad suner play wi' a tay spune!". A leading Danish linguist is still hard at work translating the sentence.

Snead
S. J. "Slamming Sammy" won every major golf tournament except the U.S. Open. In the 1979 Quad Cities Open, Illinois, he scored a 66, an incredible round, being under his age at the time. He once declared "When you leave the United States you're just camping out", a remark which led to him being named "Lemon of the Year" by the British Hotel Union.

Stroke
A stroke is the forward movement of the club made with the intention of striking at and moving the ball. Air shots where no connection is made must still be counted (unless not observed by your opponent).

Shank
A stroke where the ball is struck with the neck of the club, causing it to fly off at an acute and uncontrolled angle. This sounds difficult to achieve but most weekend golfers are expert at it.

Sharwood
Maurice Stanley — Amateur who lost 31 balls in 36 holes over the 'Old' Course at Fanling Golf Club on 26th May 1976. Had it not been for the 31 penalty strokes he incurred he would have had a near perfect card

Splash
What Jerry Pate made in June '81 after winning the Danny Thomas Classic. Elated, he dived fully clothed into a water hazard by the 18th hole scoring 6.3 on the Olympic Scale.

Shade, R.D.B.M.
Scottish professional who was awarded the M.B.E. in 1967 for having more initials than any other golfer.

Sierra Leone
The Freetown Club was founded in 1904 and originally had nine holes. It now has 12. No doubt they'll get around to finishing it one day.

Scottish foursome
Another quaint American term for the game which is simply called a 'foursome' everywhere else. In the U.S. the 'foursome' has the same meaning as 'four-ball' anywhere else. Confusing race, Americans.

Sarazen, 'Gene'
Always wore plus-fours or knicker-bockers when playing. Having won the U.S. Open in 1922 he failed to qualify for the British Open at Troon the following year. He vowed to return "even if he had to swim". He won it in 1932.

Like hell its a lost ball! at $2.50 a time?!!

Scotch croquet

A derogatory name given to golf in the United States around 1890 and just one more reason why Americans have never understood or been able to play the game well.

Sicily, golf in

Before the Second World War there was a nine-hole course at Palermo. In 1943 German fliers made enough holes around Palermo for a hundred or more courses.

Skulled

What happened to Edward Sladwick's caddie at Durban on 28th September 1913. The unfortunate lad was struck on the head by a drive which rebounded 75 yards — a world record.

Stay regular. Eat Californian prunes. It's a moving experience.

"THE PERFECT SWING"

Scottish professional Hamish McFrigg shows the completely natural and grooved swing which is the hallmark of his game - - - - this can be yours!!!

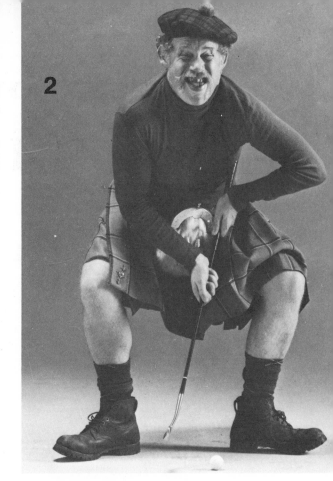

1 Be confident — positive — you can hit it a mile
2 Addressing the ball
3 Slowly back — wrists cocked — pause at the top
4 Unleash the awesome power of the downswing
5 Bring the hips through smoothly to the crucial impact point

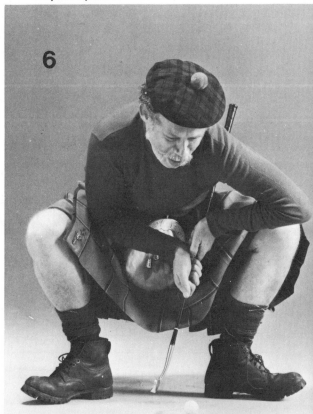

6 Optimum concentration on
   impact - - -
7 Controlled follow through - - -
   hands high — weight
   evenly balanced - - - perfect
   rhythm - - -
8 **How the hell could I miss
   that putt!!**

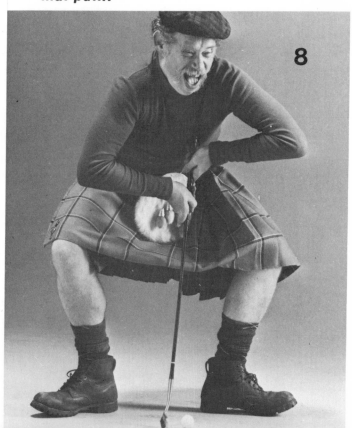

Tactics.
In the 1981 Sammy Davis Jnr. Greater Hartford Open, Jim Simons opened with a nine under par 62 and commented that he still had a long way to go. He was right . . . 60 more holes in fact. Deadlocked with Howard Twitty and going into a sudden-death playoff, Simons said: "Howard has a reputation for being a big eater. If I take him past dinner time I'll have him". An hour and a half later he commented "I was wrong". Twitty had a 5 course lunch and won by four strokes.

Tait, Rev. J. T.
This Scottish minister climbed to the top of the Great Pyramid of Giza with a golf ball in his pocket and, using an umbrella as a club, drove off. (In a fit of peak?). Only an Englishman would take an umbrella to Egypt and only a Scot would climb a bloody pyramid with it.

"It's so hot the oil is even dripping off the ancestral portraits" — Lee Trevino, British Open at Muirfield 1972.

Trevino, Lee
Mexican American who borrowed the last of his wife's savings to enter the 1968 U.S. Open. A week later he was a millionaire. He electrified the huge crowd then and also in 1975 when he was struck by lighting in the Western Open.

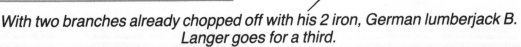

With two branches already chopped off with his 2 iron, German lumberjack B. Langer goes for a third.

SuperMex Lee Trevino beats Jack Nicklaus in the 1974 USPGA at Tanglewood Golf Club, North Carolina.

During the practice rounds for the 1981 Memorial Tournament in the U.S.A., the legendary Gene Littler asked Miller Barber to help him with his swing. Said Barber: "That's like trying to tell Stradivari how to play the violin".

THE **ABC** OF GOLF

Unplayable lie
A situation where a golfer is unable to get a shot away.

Unpliable lay
A situation where a golfer is unable to get a shot away.

"Golf is a test of temper, a trial of honour, a revealler of character"

Idi Amin interviewed at the Kampala Golf and Country Club after the mysterious disappearance of the Chief Justice of Uganda.

Unplayable
American journalist Jim Millar, playing the 16th at Delhi, the hazardous "Monkey Hole" had his ball eaten like a marshmallow by a bull rhesus monkey. He declared the ball both lost and unplayable and continued without penalty.

U.S. Masters
Is traditionally held during the first week of April. When a committee member pointed out that the proposed fixture date clashed with the celebration of Holy Week Clifford Roberts replied "Then change Easter".

Ugandan golf
The game was very big in Uganda until Idi Amin ate the pro at the Jina course. One of the local rules at Jina reads, 'On the green, a ball interfered with by a hippo footmark may be lifted and placed not nearer the hole, without penalty'. There were no local rules governing the devouring of club professionals or caddies.

Dis Scodlund are da plaze for tartan

Dat Goddam Scodish porridge Not even dat castor oil'l shift dat stuff.

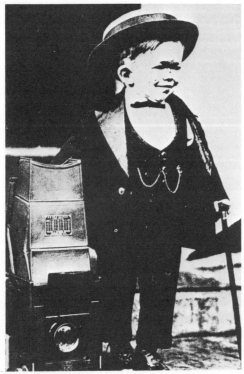

American golf photographer Eric Eiffel whose pictures of putting surfaces and famous feet are unique in the sport.

Bob Hope's Greek caddie at the Athens Open 1978.

THE **ABC** OF GOLF

Vardon, Harry

The Bjorn Borg of Golf he won six British Opens whilst perfecting the "overlap" grip named after him. His record remains intact despite assaults by Braid and Taylor, Vardon's contemporaries, and Peter Thompson of Australia.

Von Nida, Norman

Despite having his knee broken in 1931 by a trick golfer who mis-hit and shattered his leg whilst attempting to drive a ball from that unlikely tee, he went on to become one of Australias finest golfers. Was involved in a punch-up with Henry Ransom whilst playing the American Tournament circuit. Having tried boxing retired to breed racehorses in Australia.

Harry Vardon, hampered by a badly made suit is beaten by Ted Ray in the 1912 British Open at Muirfield.

THE **ABC** OF GOLF

Weiskopf, Tom

American professional, who was leading a Canadian tournament by four strokes. Threw the tournament, his clubs, caddie, the referee, a taco stand, two T.V. crews and a lockerroom into a water hazard after he had been distracted by a clicking camera. Has now matured and has won the British Open.

Waites, Brian (U.K.)

On 25 February 1982 this British player slammed an almighty three wood out of a bunker on Hong Kong's Composite Course and almost won a U.S. $20,000 car. Almost. The car was up for grabs for an eagle on the 18th.

His shot carried 200 yards, clearing a menacing pond and a deep potbunker to hit the flagstick. Unhappily, the ball missed the hole and fell four feet away.

"That was the greatest shot of my life," Waites said. He then missed the putt.

Contest: Pick the three prize winners in the John Newcombe Classic and win a personally guaranteed 'Newk' inflatable money belt.

Japan's Isao Aoki misses his tee shot completely at the Dunlop Masters in 1979, proving that Japanese people have no rhythm, co-ordination or ball sense and are only good at making TV sets and small cars.

Yips

A dreaded psychological block which affects weekend players and professionals alike, particularly when putting. The most obvious signs are trembling, blood draining from the face, clubs and bag being thrown into a bunker or water hazard.

NOTICE

This was originally one of numerous full-page paid advertisement spaces reserved by Dunlop, Slazenger and Arnold Palmer Sportswear and costing thousands of dollars a page. However we were so overwhelmed with paid editorial contributions from two wealthy would-be authors that we are now able to tell all you top companies to blow it out your ears.

Yours, offshore and tax-free

The Publishers

Bermuda

Where Are They Now?

Our editorial staff has received numerous letters from golf fans the world over asking if we know what has become of the Falkland Islands professional of the late forties and early fifties, Jimmy Mato Grosso.

Most of our readers will remember Jimmy's epic fourth place in the Tierra Del Fuego Open in 1949 when, leading the field by 17 strokes going into the final nine he was dogged by bad luck and even worse play which cost him the title and the $25.00 first-prize.

Jimmy is fondly remembered by his fellow pros for his light-hearted approach to the game, his warm, easy smile and for his wife Dolores who had enormous tits and was the best bash on the circuit.

When we last heard from this gentle and friendly old pro he was doing 15 years in a leading Buenos Aires prison after questionning the accuracy of Juan Peron's score-card.

THE **ABC** OF GOLF

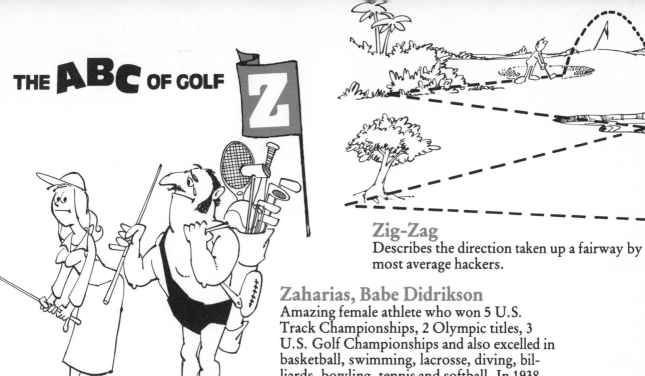

Zig-Zag
Describes the direction taken up a fairway by most average hackers.

Zaharias, Babe Didrikson
Amazing female athlete who won 5 U.S. Track Championships, 2 Olympic titles, 3 U.S. Golf Championships and also excelled in basketball, swimming, lacrosse, diving, billiards, bowling, tennis and softball. In 1938 married a Wrestler known as the Crying Greek from Cripple Creek, and thereafter excelled in the body press. Also played the mouth organ in a touring vaudeville act.

Australia's Greg Norman practices at his father's ranch down under in preparation for the 1982 Goolagong Hay Pitching Championships.

Acknowledgement

Any reference to persons living or dead is either entirely accidental or deliberate. All incidents related are either totally ficticious or based on documented fact. All text and pictures are either original creative effort or stolen. (Our sincere thanks to all those great publishing houses of the world for the vast amount of material we have used to compile this extremely successful book).

Troon, 1923. Head Greenkeeper and leading professional, Arthur Sartorial, demonstrates the latest British scrub clearing technique.